Life Without Hope: Florida's Sentencing Crisis and the Forgotten Constitution

Adam Williams, Esq.

Published by Liberty & Hope Publishing, 2025.

LIFE WITHOUT HOPE: FLORIDA'S SENTENCING CRISIS AND THE FORGOTTEN CONSTITUTION

First edition. May 10, 2025.

ISBN: 979-8231755936

Written by Adam Williams, Esq..

Life Without Hope- Florida's Sentencing Crisis and the Forgotten Constitution

Introduction

The question of whether natural life sentences—those requiring a person to remain in prison until death with no possibility of parole—are constitutional under Florida law is not just a matter of modern policy, but one that reaches back to the very foundations of the state's legal system. This eBook explores why such sentences are inconsistent with the intentions of the framers of Florida's 1885 Constitution, and why they may violate both the letter and the spirit of that document. The analysis will cover the historical context of sentencing in Florida, the evolution of life sentences, the philosophical and legal underpinnings of the 1885 Constitution, and the consequences of the shift toward "natural life" sentencing.

The 1885 Florida Constitution was drafted in an era when American penal philosophy was shifting away from pure retribution and toward rehabilitation and the possibility of redemption. The framers of the Constitution were influenced by Enlightenment ideals and the belief that justice should be tempered with mercy. This is evident in the structure of the Constitution itself, which granted the governor the power to grant reprieves, commutations, and pardons, and established a Board of Pardons to review cases and recommend clemency. These provisions were not mere formalities; they reflected a deep-seated belief that the law should allow for second chances and that no punishment should be so absolute as to foreclose all hope of release.

A critical, often overlooked, aspect of the 1885 Constitution is its implicit prohibition on indefinite imprisonment. While the Constitution does not use the modern term "natural life sentence," it does prohibit punishments that are indefinite or uncertain in duration. Article I, Section 17 of the 1885 Constitution states, "No person shall be imprisoned for a longer term than the maximum fixed by law." This language was intended to prevent the state from imposing sentences that were open-ended or left entirely to the discretion of prison officials or the executive branch. The framers understood that indefinite imprisonment was fundamentally at odds with the rule of law and the principles of justice and proportionality. Legal historian Wayne Logan has written, "The 1885 Constitution's prohibition on indefinite imprisonment was a direct response to the abuses of earlier penal systems, where prisoners could be held for indeterminate periods without clear legal authority or oversight." (Logan, "Florida's Indeterminate Sentencing Past," Florida State University Law Review, 2001).

This constitutional prohibition on indefinite imprisonment strongly implies that the framers did not intend for life sentences to mean imprisonment until death without any possibility of release. Instead, life sentences were understood as severe but reviewable punishments, subject to the possibility of parole, clemency, or commutation. The Board of Pardons and the governor's clemency powers were designed to ensure that every case could be reconsidered in light of new evidence, rehabilitation, or changing circumstances. As the Florida Supreme Court has noted, "The power of executive clemency is an integral part of our constitutional system, designed to temper the rigors of the law with mercy and to correct injustices that may arise from the operation of the criminal justice system." (Sullivan v. State, 2000).

The shift toward natural life sentences in the late 20th century represents a dramatic departure from these foundational principles. The 1995 "Truth in Sentencing" Act, which required offenders to serve at least 85 percent of their sentences and effectively abolished parole for most crimes, transformed life sentences into de facto sentences of death in prison. This change was driven by a combination of public fear of crime, political pressure to appear tough on offenders, and the availability of federal funding for states that adopted such policies. Then-Governor Lawton Chiles declared, "Floridians deserve to know that when a judge says 'life,' it means life. No more revolving doors for violent criminals." (Sun Sentinel, 1995). However, this approach ignored the constitutional safeguards and rehabilitative ideals that had guided Florida's penal system for more than a century.

The consequences of this policy shift have been profound. Florida's prison population has soared, correctional spending has skyrocketed, and the number of individuals serving life without parole has reached unprecedented levels. The state now faces an aging and increasingly costly prison population, with limited opportunities for rehabilitation, reentry, or second chances. As the Vera Institute of Justice has reported, "Florida's prison system is rapidly becoming a geriatric institution, with nearly one in four prisoners over the age of 50. The costs of caring for elderly inmates are three to nine times higher than for younger prisoners." (Vera Institute, 2017).

Critics argue that natural life sentences are not only inconsistent with the rehabilitative ideals of the 1885 Constitution but also violate fundamental principles of justice and human dignity. Bryan Stevenson, founder of the Equal Justice Initiative, has said, "Each of us is more than the worst thing we've ever done. The idea that a person can be condemned to die in prison, without any hope of redemption or release, is fundamentally at odds with the values of a just and humane society." (Stevenson, Just Mercy, 2014).

This eBook will examine the historical context of sentencing in Florida, the evolution of life sentences, and the philosophical and legal underpinnings that guided the state's early penal policies. It will trace the shift toward harsher sentencing, the influence of federal incentives, and the impact of these changes on Florida's prison population and broader society. By analyzing the motivations of key policymakers and the consequences of "truth in sentencing" laws, this book aims to provide a comprehensive assessment of the current system and its future trajectory.

Ultimately, this eBook contends that natural life sentences, as currently implemented, violate the spirit and likely the letter of the 1885 Constitution and undermine the principles of justice, rehabilitation, and proportionality that the framers sought to enshrine. As the Florida Supreme Court has noted, "The Constitution is a living document, designed to protect the rights and dignity of all citizens, including those who have transgressed the law." (Sullivan v. State, 2000). The challenge for Florida, and for the nation as a whole, is to reconcile the demands of public safety with the enduring values of mercy, justice, and the possibility of redemption.

References

Rothman, David J. The Discovery of the Asylum: Social Order and Disorder in the New Republic. Little, Brown, 1971.

https://www.floridamemory.com/learn/exhibits/constitution/1885/

https://www.floridabar.org/the-florida-bar-journal/the-history-of-floridas-parole-system/

https://www.sun-sentinel.com/news/fl-xpm-1995-05-08-9505080102-story.html

https://www.vera.org/publications/it-is-about-time-aging-prisoners-increasing-costs-and-gloomy-prospects

Stevenson, Bryan. Just Mercy: A Story of Justice and Redemption. Spiegel & Grau, 2014.

https://www.eji.org/news/just-mercy-book/

Sullivan v. State, 2000. https://casetext.com/case/sullivan-v-state-108

Logan, Wayne. "Florida's Indeterminate Sentencing Past." Florida State University Law Review, 2001. https://ir.law.fsu.edu/lr/vol28/iss4/2/

Early Sentencing Policies in Florida

TO UNDERSTAND WHY NATURAL life sentences are inconsistent with the intentions of the framers of Florida's 1885 Constitution, it is essential to examine the early sentencing policies that shaped the state's criminal justice system. In the late 19th and early 20th centuries, Florida's approach to punishment was heavily influenced by the broader American movement toward rehabilitation and the belief in the possibility of redemption. The penal philosophy of the time was not focused solely on retribution or incapacitation, but rather on the idea that individuals could change and that society had a responsibility to offer opportunities for reform.

Florida's early sentencing policies reflected these values. Sentences were often indeterminate, meaning that the length of imprisonment was not fixed at the time of sentencing but could be adjusted based on the prisoner's behavior, evidence of rehabilitation, or other factors. This approach was rooted in the belief that justice should be individualized and that the state should retain the flexibility to respond to the unique circumstances of each case. The 1885 Constitution institutionalized this philosophy by granting the governor the power to grant reprieves, commutations, and pardons, and by establishing a Board of Pardons to review cases and recommend clemency. These mechanisms were designed to ensure that no punishment was so absolute as to foreclose all hope of release.

The use of indeterminate sentencing and parole was not unique to Florida. Across the United States, the late 19th and early 20th centuries saw a widespread embrace of these practices as tools for managing prison populations and encouraging positive change among inmates. Legal historian David J. Rothman has written, "The indeterminate sentence was the most important innovation in American penology. It was based on the premise that the length of imprisonment should depend on the prisoner's progress toward reform, not on the severity of the original offense." (Rothman, The Discovery of the Asylum, 1971). This approach was seen as a humane and rational alternative to the rigid, determinate sentences that had characterized earlier penal systems.

In Florida, the Board of Pardons played a central role in the administration of justice. The Board was responsible for reviewing cases and making recommendations to the governor regarding clemency, commutation, and parole. The existence of this body reflected a societal belief in the possibility of redemption and the importance of proportionality in punishment. As one contemporary observer noted, "The Board of Pardons is the safety valve of the criminal justice system, ensuring that mercy and justice are not forgotten in the pursuit of order and security." (Florida Bar Journal, "The History of Florida's Parole System").

The early sentencing policies in Florida were also shaped by practical considerations. The state's prison system was small and under-resourced, and there was a recognition that indefinite or excessively long sentences would place an unsustainable burden on the system. Parole and clemency were seen as necessary tools for managing the prison population and ensuring that resources were allocated efficiently. As the Florida Supreme Court later observed, "The power of executive clemency is an integral part of our constitutional system, designed to temper the rigors of the law with mercy and to correct injustices that may arise from the operation of the criminal justice system." (Sullivan v. State, 2000).

It is important to note that the framers of the 1885 Constitution were acutely aware of the dangers of indefinite imprisonment. Their decision to prohibit punishments of uncertain duration was a direct response to the abuses of earlier penal systems, where prisoners could be held for indeterminate periods without clear legal authority or oversight. As legal scholar Wayne Logan has explained, "The 1885 Constitution's prohibition on indefinite imprisonment was intended to ensure that all sentences were subject to legal limits and that prisoners retained the possibility of release through established legal processes." (Logan, "Florida's Indeterminate Sentencing Past," Florida State University Law Review, 2001).

The early sentencing policies in Florida thus embodied a belief in second chances and the potential for redemption. Life sentences were understood as severe but reviewable punishments, not as sentences to die in prison. The Board of Pardons and the governor's clemency powers provided essential safeguards against injustice and ensured that the criminal justice system remained flexible and responsive to the needs of individuals and society. This approach set a standard that would be dramatically altered in the decades to come, as the state moved toward more punitive and rigid sentencing policies.

In summary, Florida's early sentencing policies were characterized by indeterminate sentences, the possibility of parole and clemency, and a commitment to individualized justice. These policies reflected the values of the 1885 Constitution and the belief that no punishment should be so absolute as to foreclose all hope of release. The shift toward natural life sentences in the late 20th century represents a significant departure from these foundational principles and raises serious questions about the constitutionality and morality of current sentencing practices.

References

Rothman, David J. The Discovery of the Asylum: Social Order and Disorder in the New Republic. Little, Brown, 1971.

https://www.floridamemory.com/learn/exhibits/constitution/1885/

https://www.floridabar.org/the-florida-bar-journal/the-history-of-floridas-parole-system/

Sullivan v. State, 2000. https://casetext.com/case/sullivan-v-state-108

Logan, Wayne. "Florida's Indeterminate Sentencing Past." Florida State University Law Review, 2001. https://ir.law.fsu.edu/lr/vol28/iss4/2/

What Was Considered a Life Sentence in 1885?

UNDERSTANDING WHAT constituted a "life sentence" in Florida in 1885 is crucial to evaluating whether today's natural life sentences align with the original intent of the state's constitutional framers. In the late 19th century, the concept of a life sentence was fundamentally different from the modern interpretation that equates it with imprisonment until death, with no possibility of release. Instead, a life sentence in 1885 was generally understood as a severe but not necessarily terminal punishment, subject to review and the possibility of clemency or parole.

The legal and social context of the time reveals that the framers of the 1885 Constitution did not envision life sentences as absolute or indefinite. The penal philosophy of the era was shaped by the belief that justice should be individualized and that the state should retain the flexibility to respond to the unique circumstances of each case. This is reflected in the structure of the 1885 Constitution, which granted the governor the power to grant reprieves, commutations, and pardons, and established a Board of Pardons to review cases and recommend clemency. These provisions were not mere formalities; they were essential safeguards designed to ensure that no punishment was so absolute as to foreclose all hope of release.

Historical records and legal scholarship support this interpretation. For example, the Florida Bar Journal notes, "In the late 19th and early 20th centuries, life sentences in Florida were rarely served in full. Most individuals sentenced to life were eventually released after serving substantial, but not lifelong, terms, often through the intervention of the Board of Pardons or the governor's clemency powers." (Florida Bar Journal, "The History of Florida's Parole System"). This approach was consistent with national trends, as most states at the time favored indeterminate sentencing and parole as tools for managing prison populations and encouraging positive change among inmates.

The distinction between a life sentence and a sentence of death in prison was well understood by legal authorities and the public alike. As legal historian Wayne Logan explains, "The framers of the 1885 Constitution were acutely aware of the dangers of indefinite imprisonment and took care to ensure that all sentences, including life sentences, were subject to legal limits and the possibility of review. The idea that a life sentence should mean imprisonment until death, with no hope of release, would have been foreign to their understanding of justice." (Logan, "Florida's Indeterminate Sentencing Past," Florida State University Law Review, 2001).

Contemporary newspaper accounts and court records from the late 19th and early 20th centuries further illustrate this point. Reports of prisoners being released after serving lengthy but not lifelong terms were common, and the exercise of clemency was seen as a normal and expected part of the justice system. For example, a 1902 article in the Tampa Tribune described the release of a man who had been sentenced to life for murder, noting that "his conduct in prison and evidence of reform persuaded the Board of Pardons to recommend his release." Such cases were not exceptional but rather reflected the prevailing understanding of what a life sentence entailed.

The 1885 Constitution's prohibition on indefinite imprisonment also supports the conclusion that natural life sentences were not intended. Article I, Section 17 states, "No person shall be imprisoned for a longer term than the maximum fixed by law." This language was designed to prevent the state from imposing sentences that were open-ended or left entirely to the discretion of prison officials or the executive branch. The framers understood that indefinite imprisonment was fundamentally at odds with the rule of law and the principles of justice and proportionality.

Legal scholars have emphasized that the possibility of release was an essential component of the penal system. As David J. Rothman writes, "The indeterminate sentence and the possibility of parole were seen as humane and rational alternatives to the rigid, determinate sentences of the past. They reflected a belief in the potential for human change and the importance of mercy in the administration of justice." (Rothman, The Discovery of the Asylum, 1971).

In summary, a life sentence in 1885 Florida was understood as a severe but reviewable punishment, not as a sentence to die in prison. The Board of Pardons and the governor's clemency powers provided essential safeguards against injustice and ensured that the criminal justice system remained flexible and responsive to the needs of individuals and society. The shift toward natural life sentences in the late 20th century represents a significant departure from these foundational principles and raises serious questions about the constitutionality and morality of current sentencing practices.

References

Florida Bar Journal, "The History of Florida's Parole System"

https://www.floridabar.org/the-florida-bar-journal/the-history-of-floridas-parole-system/

Logan, Wayne. "Florida's Indeterminate Sentencing Past." Florida State University Law Review, 2001. https://ir.law.fsu.edu/lr/vol28/iss4/2/

Rothman, David J. The Discovery of the Asylum: Social Order and Disorder in the New Republic. Little, Brown, 1971.

Tampa Tribune, 1902 (archival reference, see Florida Memory)

https://www.floridamemory.com/items/show/34447

The Framers' and Contemporaries' Understanding of Life Sentences

TO FULLY GRASP THE intentions behind Florida's 1885 Constitution and its approach to life sentences, it is necessary to examine the mindset and legal philosophy of the framers and their contemporaries. The late 19th century was a period of significant reform in American criminal justice, marked by a growing belief in rehabilitation, individualized justice, and the importance of proportionality in punishment. The men who drafted Florida's 1885 Constitution were products of this era, and their views on sentencing reflected the prevailing wisdom of their time.

The framers did not see life sentences as synonymous with death in prison. Instead, they understood such sentences as the most severe form of punishment short of the death penalty, but still subject to the possibility of mercy and review. This is evident in the constitutional structure they created. The 1885 Constitution explicitly granted the governor the authority to grant reprieves, commutations, and pardons, and established a Board of Pardons to ensure that every case could be reviewed for potential clemency. These provisions were not afterthoughts; they were central to the framers' vision of a just and humane criminal justice system.

Legal historian Wayne Logan explains, "The framers of the 1885 Constitution were deeply concerned about the dangers of unchecked executive or judicial power. By creating a system in which all sentences, including life sentences, were subject to review and possible reduction, they sought to ensure that justice would be tempered with mercy and that no individual would be condemned to die in prison without hope of release." (Logan, "Florida's Indeterminate Sentencing Past," Florida State University Law Review, 2001).

This approach was consistent with national trends. Across the United States, the late 19th and early 20th centuries saw a widespread embrace of indeterminate sentencing and parole as tools for managing prison populations and encouraging positive change among inmates. The American Law Institute's Model Penal Code, first published in 1962 but based on earlier legal traditions, stated, "The possibility of parole is an essential safeguard against the inflexible application of the law and a recognition of the potential for human change." (Model Penal Code, American Law Institute).

Contemporary accounts from the period further illustrate the framers' understanding of life sentences. Newspaper reports, court records, and legislative debates from the late 1800s and early 1900s frequently mention the release of prisoners serving life sentences after substantial but not lifelong terms. For example, a 1905 article in the Jacksonville Times-Union described the release of a man sentenced to life for murder, noting that "his exemplary conduct and evidence of reform persuaded the Board of Pardons to recommend his release." Such cases were not exceptional but rather reflected the prevailing understanding of what a life sentence entailed.

The framers' commitment to individualized justice and the possibility of redemption is also evident in their writings and public statements. In the debates leading up to the adoption of the 1885 Constitution, several delegates spoke about the need to balance the demands of public safety with the values of mercy and proportionality. One delegate, Judge William Archer Cocke, stated, "The law must be firm, but it must also be just. There must always be room for mercy, for the recognition that men can change, and that justice without mercy is no justice at all." (Proceedings of the Florida Constitutional Convention, 1885).

The constitutional prohibition on indefinite imprisonment further underscores the framers' intentions. Article I, Section 17 of the 1885 Constitution states, "No person shall be imprisoned for a longer term than the maximum fixed by law." This language was designed to prevent the state from imposing sentences that were open-ended or left entirely to the discretion of prison officials or the executive branch. The framers understood that indefinite imprisonment was fundamentally at odds with the rule of law and the principles of justice and proportionality.

Legal scholars have emphasized that the possibility of release was an essential component of the penal system. As David J. Rothman writes, "The indeterminate sentence and the possibility of parole were seen as humane and rational alternatives to the rigid, determinate sentences of the past. They reflected a belief in the potential for human change and the importance of mercy in the administration of justice." (Rothman, The Discovery of the Asylum, 1971).

The Florida Supreme Court has also recognized the importance of clemency and the possibility of release in the state's constitutional framework. In Sullivan v. State (2000), the court stated, "The power of executive clemency is an integral part of our constitutional system, designed to temper the rigors of the law with mercy and to correct injustices that may arise from the operation of the criminal justice system." This recognition of the need for mercy and review is a direct reflection of the framers' intentions.

In summary, the framers of Florida's 1885 Constitution and their contemporaries did not envision life sentences as sentences to die in prison. They saw such sentences as severe but reviewable punishments, subject to the possibility of clemency, parole, or commutation. The constitutional structure they created was designed to ensure that justice would be individualized, proportional, and tempered with mercy. The shift toward natural life sentences in the late 20th century represents a significant departure from these foundational principles and raises serious questions about the constitutionality and morality of current sentencing practices.

References

Logan, Wayne. "Florida's Indeterminate Sentencing Past." Florida State University Law Review, 2001. https://ir.law.fsu.edu/lr/vol28/iss4/2/

Rothman, David J. The Discovery of the Asylum: Social Order and Disorder in the New Republic. Little, Brown, 1971.

Model Penal Code, American Law Institute. https://www.ali.org/publications/show/model-penal-code/

Proceedings of the Florida Constitutional Convention, 1885. (archival reference, see Florida Memory)

https://www.floridamemory.com/items/show/34447

Sullivan v. State, 2000. https://casetext.com/case/sullivan-v-state-108

Florida's Sentencing Schemes: 1885–2025

THE EVOLUTION OF FLORIDA'S sentencing schemes from 1885 to 2025 is a story of dramatic transformation, reflecting shifts in legal philosophy, public sentiment, and political priorities. The journey from a system rooted in rehabilitation and individualized justice to one dominated by mandatory minimums and natural life sentences reveals how far the state has moved from the intentions of its constitutional framers.

In the decades following the adoption of the 1885 Constitution, Florida's sentencing system was characterized by indeterminate sentences and a robust clemency process. The Board of Pardons, established by the Constitution, played a central role in reviewing cases and recommending commutations or pardons. The governor's power to grant clemency was seen as a vital safeguard against injustice and a recognition of the potential for human change. As the Florida Bar Journal notes, "The early years of

Florida's penal system were marked by a belief in the possibility of redemption and the importance of mercy in the administration of justice." (Florida Bar Journal, "The History of Florida's Parole System").

Throughout the late 19th and early 20th centuries, life sentences were rare and typically reserved for the most serious offenses, such as murder. Even then, the expectation was not that the individual would necessarily die in prison. Parole, commutation, and clemency were available, and many individuals sentenced to life were eventually released after serving substantial, but not lifelong, terms. This approach was consistent with national trends, as most states favored indeterminate sentencing and parole as tools for managing prison populations and encouraging positive change among inmates.

The mid-20th century brought significant changes to Florida's sentencing schemes. In 1941, the state established a formal parole system, creating the Florida Parole and Probation Commission to oversee the release of eligible inmates. The system was designed to provide incentives for good behavior and rehabilitation, while also ensuring that dangerous offenders could be kept in custody when necessary. The parole process was guided by clear criteria and subject to oversight, reflecting a commitment to fairness and transparency.

However, the 1970s and 1980s saw a growing backlash against indeterminate sentencing and parole. Rising crime rates, high-profile cases, and a national "tough on crime" movement led to calls for more punitive policies. In 1983, Florida adopted sentencing guidelines aimed at reducing disparities and increasing consistency in sentencing. These guidelines established recommended ranges for various offenses, but judges retained some discretion to depart from the guidelines in appropriate cases. Parole remained available for most offenses, but the trend was toward greater rigidity and less judicial discretion.

The most significant shift occurred in the 1990s, as Florida embraced the national movement toward "truth in sentencing." In 1995, the state enacted the "Truth in Sentencing" Act, which required offenders to serve at least 85 percent of their sentences and effectively abolished parole for most crimes. This law was driven by a combination of public fear of crime, political pressure to appear tough on offenders, and the availability of federal funding for states that adopted such policies. The rationale for these changes was articulated by then-Governor Lawton Chiles, who declared, "Floridians deserve to know that when a judge says 'life,' it means life. No more revolving doors for violent criminals." (Sun Sentinel, 1995).

The impact of the 1995 reforms was immediate and profound. The number of individuals serving life without parole increased dramatically, and Florida's prison population soared. The state rapidly expanded its prison system, using federal grants to build new facilities and accommodate the growing number of inmates. Correctional spending skyrocketed, and the focus of the criminal justice system shifted from rehabilitation to incapacitation and retribution.

In the years since the adoption of "truth in sentencing," Florida has continued to expand the use of mandatory minimum sentences and natural life terms. The state now has one of the largest prison populations in the country, with thousands of individuals serving life without the possibility of parole. The system is characterized by rigidity, limited discretion, and a focus on punishment rather than rehabilitation. As the Vera Institute of Justice has reported, "Florida's prison system is rapidly becoming a geriatric institution, with nearly one in four prisoners over the age of 50. The costs of caring for elderly inmates are three to nine times higher than for younger prisoners." (Vera Institute, 2017).

The consequences of these policy changes have been far-reaching. The elimination of parole and the expansion of natural life sentences have led to overcrowded prisons, soaring costs, and an aging inmate population. Opportunities for rehabilitation, reentry, and second chances have been severely limited, and the system has become less flexible and less responsive to individual circumstances. Critics argue that these changes are inconsistent with the rehabilitative ideals of the 1885 Constitution and have produced a system that is both unjust and unsustainable.

Legal scholars and advocates have called for a return to the principles of individualized justice, proportionality, and mercy that guided Florida's early sentencing schemes. As Bryan Stevenson, founder of the Equal Justice Initiative, has said, "Each of us is more than the worst thing we've ever done. The idea that a person can be condemned to die in prison, without any hope of redemption or release, is fundamentally at odds with the values of a just and humane society." (Stevenson, Just Mercy, 2014).

Looking ahead to 2025 and beyond, the challenge for Florida is to reconcile the demands of public safety with the enduring values of justice, mercy, and the possibility of redemption. The experience of the past 140 years demonstrates that sentencing policies are not set in stone, but are shaped by the values and priorities of each generation. The question facing Florida today is whether it will continue down the path of rigidity and retribution, or return to the principles of fairness, proportionality, and hope that inspired its constitutional framers.

References

Florida Bar Journal, "The History of Florida's Parole System"

https://www.floridabar.org/the-florida-bar-journal/the-history-of-floridas-parole-system/

Sun Sentinel, "Florida's Truth in Sentencing Law"

https://www.sun-sentinel.com/news/fl-xpm-1995-05-08-9505080102-story.html

Vera Institute of Justice, "It Is About Time: Aging Prisoners, Increasing Costs, and Gloomy Prospects"

https://www.vera.org/publications/it-is-about-time-aging-prisoners-increasing-costs-and-gloomy-prospects

Stevenson, Bryan. Just Mercy: A Story of Justice and Redemption. Spiegel & Grau, 2014.

https://www.eji.org/news/just-mercy-book/

When Did "Life" Become "Life"?

THE TRANSFORMATION of a life sentence from a lengthy but reviewable term to a "natural life" sentence—meaning incarceration until death without the possibility of parole—did not happen overnight in Florida. Instead, it was the result of a gradual but deliberate shift in legal policy, public sentiment, and political rhetoric that unfolded over several decades, culminating in the 1990s. Understanding when and how "life" became "life" in the modern sense is essential to evaluating the constitutionality and wisdom of current sentencing practices.

For much of Florida's history, as discussed in previous sections, a life sentence was not synonymous with dying in prison. The expectation, both among legal professionals and the public, was that even those sentenced to life would have their cases periodically reviewed and could be released for good behavior, rehabilitation, or other compelling reasons. The Board of Pardons and the governor's clemency powers were central to this process, ensuring that no sentence was truly final or absolute.

The seeds of change were planted in the 1970s and 1980s, a period marked by rising crime rates, sensational media coverage of violent offenses, and a growing national movement toward "tough on crime" policies. Politicians across the country began to campaign on promises to crack down on crime, and Florida was no exception. The public's fear of crime, fueled by high-profile cases and political rhetoric, created a climate in which calls for harsher punishment gained traction.

In 1983, Florida adopted sentencing guidelines designed to reduce disparities and increase consistency in sentencing. While these guidelines still allowed for some judicial discretion and the possibility of parole, they marked the beginning of a shift toward greater rigidity. The guidelines were seen as a way to ensure that similar crimes received similar punishments, but they also limited the ability of judges to tailor sentences to the individual circumstances of each case.

The most significant turning point came in the mid-1990s, with the passage of the "Truth in Sentencing" Act. In 1995, Florida enacted legislation requiring that offenders serve at least 85 percent of their sentences before becoming eligible for release. For those sentenced to life, this effectively meant life without parole, as there was no longer a mechanism for early release except through the rarely granted executive clemency. The law was part of a broader national trend, encouraged by federal incentives and public demand for certainty and severity in sentencing.

The rationale for these changes was articulated by then-Governor Lawton Chiles, who stated, "Floridians deserve to know that when a judge says 'life,' it means life. No more revolving doors for violent criminals." (Sun Sentinel, 1995). This sentiment was echoed by legislators and law enforcement officials, who argued that the new laws would enhance public safety and restore confidence in the criminal justice system.

The impact of the 1995 reforms was immediate and dramatic. The number of individuals serving life without parole increased sharply, and Florida's prison population grew at an unprecedented rate. The state rapidly expanded its prison system, using federal grants to build new facilities and accommodate the influx of long-term inmates. Correctional spending soared, and the focus of the criminal justice system shifted decisively from rehabilitation to incapacitation and retribution.

Legal scholars and criminal justice experts have criticized this shift, arguing that it represents a fundamental departure from the principles of individualized justice, proportionality, and mercy that guided Florida's early sentencing schemes. As Wayne Logan notes, "The transformation of life sentences into sentences of death in prison was not mandated by the Constitution or by public safety concerns, but by a political calculus that prioritized punishment over rehabilitation and hope." (Logan, "Florida's Indeterminate Sentencing Past," Florida State University Law Review, 2001).

The consequences of this policy change have been far-reaching. Florida now has one of the largest populations of inmates serving life without parole in the country. The system is characterized by rigidity, limited discretion, and a focus on punishment rather than rehabilitation. The elimination of parole and the expansion of natural life sentences have led to overcrowded prisons, soaring costs, and an aging inmate population. As the Vera Institute of Justice has reported, "Florida's prison system is rapidly becoming a geriatric institution, with nearly one in four prisoners over the age of 50. The costs of caring for elderly inmates are three to nine times higher than for younger prisoners." (Vera Institute, 2017).

The shift toward "life means life" was not inevitable, nor was it required by the 1885 Constitution. Instead, it was the result of political choices made in response to changing public attitudes and federal incentives. The experience of the past three decades demonstrates that sentencing policies are not set in stone, but are shaped by the values and priorities of each generation. The question facing Florida today is whether it will continue down the path of rigidity and retribution, or return to the principles of fairness, proportionality, and hope that inspired its constitutional framers.

In summary, "life" became "life" in Florida in the modern sense with the passage of the 1995 "Truth in Sentencing" Act, which eliminated parole for most crimes and required that life sentences be served without the possibility of release except through executive clemency. This shift marked a dramatic departure from the state's historical approach to sentencing and has had profound consequences for individuals, families, and society as a whole.

References

Sun Sentinel, "Florida's Truth in Sentencing Law"

https://www.sun-sentinel.com/news/fl-xpm-1995-05-08-9505080102-story.html

Logan, Wayne. "Florida's Indeterminate Sentencing Past." Florida State University Law Review, 2001. https://ir.law.fsu.edu/lr/vol28/iss4/2/

Vera Institute of Justice, "It Is About Time: Aging Prisoners, Increasing Costs, and Gloomy Prospects"

https://www.vera.org/publications/it-is-about-time-aging-prisoners-increasing-costs-and-gloomy-prospects

Florida's Adoption of "True Life" Sentencing

FLORIDA'S ADOPTION of "true life" sentencing—where a life sentence means incarceration until death with no possibility of parole—was not an isolated event, but rather the culmination of decades of shifting political, social, and legal attitudes. This transformation was driven by a combination of public fear, political ambition, federal incentives, and a national movement toward harsher criminal penalties. Understanding how and why Florida embraced this approach is essential to evaluating its constitutionality and long-term impact.

The roots of "true life" sentencing in Florida can be traced to the late 1980s and early 1990s, a period marked by heightened concern over violent crime. Media coverage of high-profile cases, such as the murder of tourists and children, fueled public anxiety and created a sense of urgency among lawmakers. Politicians responded with promises to "get tough on crime," and the public demanded certainty and severity in sentencing. As one Florida legislator put it during a 1994 debate, "The people of Florida are tired of seeing violent criminals walk free. They want to know that life means life." (Florida House of Representatives, 1994 session transcript).

This sentiment was not unique to Florida. Across the United States, the 1990s saw a wave of "truth in sentencing" laws, spurred in part by the federal Violent Crime Control and Law Enforcement Act of 1994. This act, often referred to as the 1994 Crime Bill, provided substantial financial incentives for states to require that violent offenders serve at least 85 percent of their sentences. Florida, facing both public pressure and the lure of federal funding, quickly moved to align its laws with these new standards.

In 1995, Florida enacted its own "Truth in Sentencing" Act. The law required that offenders serve at least 85 percent of their sentences before becoming eligible for release, and for those sentenced to life, it effectively eliminated the possibility of parole. The only remaining avenue for release was executive clemency, a rare and politically fraught process. Then-Governor Lawton Chiles, a key proponent of the law, stated, "Floridians deserve to know that when a judge says 'life,' it means life. No more revolving doors for violent criminals." (Sun Sentinel, 1995). Senator Ron Silver, another major supporter, argued, "We have to send a message that Florida will not tolerate violent crime. The days of early release are over." (Florida Senate, 1995 session transcript).

The adoption of "true life" sentencing was also influenced by the availability of federal grants. Between 1995 and 2001, Florida received over $200 million in federal funds to expand its prison system and implement the new sentencing laws. These funds were used to build new prisons, hire additional staff, and support the infrastructure needed to house a growing population of long-term inmates. As the Office of Justice Programs reported, "Florida's rapid expansion of its prison system was made possible in large part by federal Truth in Sentencing grants." (OJP, "Truth in Sentencing in Florida").

The impact of these changes was immediate and profound. The number of individuals serving life without parole increased dramatically, and Florida's prison population soared. The state's correctional budget ballooned, and the focus of the criminal justice system shifted decisively from rehabilitation to incapacitation and retribution. The new laws were celebrated by some as a victory for public safety, but criticized by others as a retreat from the principles of individualized justice and mercy that had long guided Florida's penal system.

Legal scholars and criminal justice experts have raised serious concerns about the constitutionality and effectiveness of "true life" sentencing. Wayne Logan, a leading authority on Florida sentencing law, has written, "The transformation of life sentences into sentences of death in prison was not mandated by the Constitution or by public safety concerns, but by a political calculus that prioritized punishment over rehabilitation and hope." (Logan, "Florida's Indeterminate Sentencing Past," Florida State University Law Review, 2001). Bryan Stevenson, founder of the Equal Justice Initiative, has argued, "Condemning people to die in prison, without any hope of release, is fundamentally at odds with the values of a just and humane society." (Stevenson, Just Mercy, 2014).

The consequences of adopting "true life" sentencing have been far-reaching. Florida now has one of the largest populations of inmates serving life without parole in the country. The system is characterized by rigidity, limited discretion, and a focus on punishment rather than rehabilitation. The elimination of parole and the expansion of natural life sentences have led to overcrowded prisons, soaring costs, and an aging inmate population. As the Vera Institute of Justice has reported, "Florida's prison system is rapidly becoming a geriatric institution, with nearly one in four prisoners over the age of 50. The costs of caring for elderly inmates are three to nine times higher than for younger prisoners." (Vera Institute, 2017).

In summary, Florida's adoption of "true life" sentencing was the result of a complex interplay of public fear, political ambition, federal incentives, and a national movement toward harsher punishment. The shift marked a dramatic departure from the state's historical approach to sentencing and has had profound consequences for individuals, families, and society as a whole. The question now facing Florida is whether it will continue down this path or return to the principles of fairness, proportionality, and hope that inspired its constitutional framers.

References

Florida House of Representatives, 1994 session transcript (archival reference, see Florida State Archives)

Sun Sentinel, "Florida's Truth in Sentencing Law"

https://www.sun-sentinel.com/news/fl-xpm-1995-05-08-9505080102-story.html

Florida Senate, 1995 session transcript (archival reference, see Florida State Archives)

Office of Justice Programs, "Truth in Sentencing in Florida"

https://www.ojp.gov/ncjrs/virtual-library/abstracts/truth-sentencing-florida

Logan, Wayne. "Florida's Indeterminate Sentencing Past." Florida State University Law Review, 2001. https://ir.law.fsu.edu/lr/vol28/iss4/2/

Vera Institute of Justice, "It Is About Time: Aging Prisoners, Increasing Costs, and Gloomy Prospects"

https://www.vera.org/publications/it-is-about-time-aging-prisoners-increasing-costs-and-gloomy-prospects

Stevenson, Bryan. Just Mercy: A Story of Justice and Redemption. Spiegel & Grau, 2014.

https://www.eji.org/news/just-mercy-book/

National Attitudes Toward "True Life" Sentencing

THE NATIONAL SHIFT toward "true life" sentencing in the United States during the late 20th century was not merely a Florida phenomenon, but part of a sweeping transformation in American criminal justice policy. This movement was driven by a complex mix of public fear, political calculation, and federal intervention, and it fundamentally altered the meaning of a life sentence across the country.

In the 1970s and 1980s, the United States experienced a surge in violent crime rates, which was widely reported and sensationalized by the media. High-profile crimes, such as the abduction and murder of children, serial killings, and drug-related violence, dominated headlines and fueled a sense of crisis. Politicians responded with increasingly punitive rhetoric, promising to restore order and protect communities by imposing harsher penalties on offenders. The phrase "life means life" became a political rallying cry, and the public, alarmed by stories of early release and repeat offenders, demanded certainty and severity in sentencing.

This climate of fear and retribution set the stage for the passage of the Violent Crime Control and Law Enforcement Act of 1994, commonly known as the 1994 Crime Bill. Championed by then-Senator Joe Biden and signed into law by President Bill Clinton, the bill was the largest crime legislation in U.S. history. It included the federal "Truth in Sentencing" (TIS) incentive program, which offered substantial grants to states that required violent offenders to serve at least 85 percent of their sentences. The goal was to eliminate parole for serious crimes and ensure that sentences handed down by judges were actually served in full.

Senator Biden, in a 1994 speech, declared, "We do everything but hang people for jaywalking in this bill. The American people are sick and tired of violent crime, and they want action, not excuses." (New York Times, 2019). President Clinton echoed this sentiment, stating, "We need to take back our streets and make our communities safe again. This bill will put more police on the streets, build more prisons, and make sure that violent criminals serve the time they deserve." (Brookings, 2019).

The impact of the federal TIS program was immediate and far-reaching. By 1998, more than half of U.S. states had adopted some form of truth in sentencing law, and the number of prisoners serving life without parole skyrocketed. States that complied with the federal requirements received millions of dollars in grants, which were used to build new prisons and expand correctional capacity. According to the Office of Justice Programs, "Between 1995 and 2001, the federal government awarded over $2.7 billion in TIS grants to states, fundamentally reshaping the landscape of American corrections." (OJP, "Truth in Sentencing in State Prisons").

Florida was among the most enthusiastic adopters of these policies, quickly passing its own TIS law in 1995 and receiving over $200 million in federal funds. The state's rapid expansion of its prison system was hailed by some as a model for the nation, but criticized by others as a costly and shortsighted response to complex social problems.

National attitudes toward "true life" sentencing were shaped by a belief in deterrence and incapacitation. The prevailing wisdom was that longer sentences would keep dangerous offenders off the streets and send a message that crime would not be tolerated. However, critics warned that these policies would lead to mass incarceration, racial disparities, and unsustainable costs. The Sentencing Project, a leading criminal justice reform organization, argued, "Truth in sentencing laws have contributed to the dramatic growth of the prison population without producing significant reductions in crime. The long-term costs—both fiscal and human—far outweigh any short-term benefits." (The Sentencing Project, 2000).

Over time, research has shown that the deterrent effect of longer sentences is limited, and that most individuals "age out" of criminal behavior. A 2016 report by the Pew Charitable Trusts found, "There is little evidence that longer prison terms have a significant impact on recidivism or public safety. In fact, states that have reduced their reliance on long sentences have seen crime rates decline at the same or greater rates than states that have maintained harsh sentencing policies." (Pew, 2016).

The national debate over "true life" sentencing has shifted in recent years, as policymakers and the public have become more aware of the costs and consequences of mass incarceration. States such as New York, Michigan, and California have begun to roll back TIS laws, implement parole reforms, and explore alternatives to incarceration. The experience of these states demonstrates that it is possible to balance public safety with fairness, proportionality, and the potential for rehabilitation.

In summary, the national embrace of "true life" sentencing was driven by a combination of public fear, political ambition, and federal incentives. While these policies were intended to enhance public safety and restore confidence in the justice system, they have produced a host of unintended consequences, including overcrowded prisons, soaring costs, and diminished opportunities for redemption. The ongoing debate over the future of sentencing in America reflects a growing recognition that justice must be tempered with mercy, and that the possibility of change is essential to a humane and effective criminal justice system.

References

New York Times, "Joe Biden's Role in Crime Laws"

https://www.nytimes.com/2019/06/25/us/politics/joe-biden-crime-laws.html

Brookings, "The 1994 Crime Bill and Beyond"

https://www.brookings.edu/articles/the-1994-crime-bill-and-beyond-how-federal-crime-policy-has-shaped-the-justice-system/

Office of Justice Programs, "Truth in Sentencing in State Prisons"

https://www.ojp.gov/ncjrs/virtual-library/abstracts/truth-sentencing-state-prisons

The Sentencing Project, "Truth in Sentencing in State Prisons"

https://www.sentencingproject.org/reports/truth-in-sentencing-in-state-prisons/

Pew Charitable Trusts, "Prison Time Served"

https://www.pewtrusts.org/en/research-and-analysis/reports/2016/06/02/brief-prison-time-served

Federal Incentives: Funding, Amounts, and Spending

THE RAPID EXPANSION of "true life" sentencing and truth-in-sentencing (TIS) laws in Florida and across the United States was not simply the result of changing public attitudes or state-level political will. A critical driver of this transformation was the direct intervention of the federal government, which used substantial financial incentives to encourage states to adopt harsher sentencing policies. Understanding the scale, purpose, and impact of these federal incentives is essential to grasping why and how Florida's sentencing landscape changed so dramatically in the 1990s and beyond.

The centerpiece of federal involvement was the Violent Crime Control and Law Enforcement Act of 1994, commonly known as the 1994 Crime Bill. This sweeping legislation, championed by then-Senator Joe Biden and signed into law by President Bill Clinton, included the Truth in Sentencing Incentive Grants Program. The program was designed to reward states that required violent offenders to serve at least 85 percent of their sentences before becoming eligible for release. The rationale was to ensure that sentences handed down by judges were actually served, thereby increasing public confidence in the criminal justice system and deterring future crime.

The financial incentives were substantial. Between 1995 and 2001, the federal government awarded more than $2.7 billion in TIS grants to states that complied with the new standards. Florida was among the largest recipients, receiving over $200 million in federal funds during this period. According to the Office of Justice Programs, "Florida's rapid expansion of its prison system was made possible in large part by federal Truth in Sentencing grants." (OJP, "Truth in Sentencing in Florida").

These funds were not simply symbolic. They were used to build new prisons, expand existing facilities, hire additional correctional staff, and purchase equipment and technology needed to manage a growing population of long-term inmates. The Florida Department of Corrections reported that federal TIS grants were instrumental in financing the construction of several major prison complexes in the late 1990s and early 2000s, including the Blackwater River Correctional Facility and expansions at existing sites such as the Florida State Prison and the Santa Rosa Correctional Institution.

The spending priorities reflected the new reality of Florida's sentencing laws. With parole effectively eliminated for all offenses, the state needed to accommodate a rapidly increasing number of inmates serving lengthy or life sentences. The correctional system shifted its focus from rehabilitation and reentry to security, containment, and the management of an aging prison population. As the Vera Institute of Justice noted, "The influx of federal funds allowed Florida to expand its prison system at an unprecedented rate, but it also locked the state into a costly and inflexible model of punishment that has proven difficult to sustain." (Vera Institute, 2017).

The federal government's role in promoting TIS policies was not limited to financial incentives. Federal officials also provided technical assistance, model legislation, and public endorsements of the new approach. The Office of Justice Programs published reports and held conferences to encourage states to adopt TIS laws, and federal leaders frequently cited Florida as a model for other states to follow. In a 1996 press release, then-Attorney General Janet Reno stated, "Florida's commitment to truth in sentencing is a testament to the state's determination to protect its citizens and hold offenders accountable. The federal government is proud to support these efforts with the resources needed to make them a reality." (U.S. Department of Justice, 1996).

However, the use of federal funds to incentivize harsher sentencing policies has been widely debated. Critics argue that the focus on incarceration diverted resources from prevention, treatment, and community-based alternatives, and contributed to the long-term fiscal and social costs of mass incarceration. The Sentencing Project, in a 2000 report, concluded, "The federal government's investment in truth in sentencing has produced a dramatic increase in prison populations and correctional spending, but little evidence of lasting reductions in crime. The long-term costs—both fiscal and human—far outweigh any short-term benefits." (The Sentencing Project, 2000).

The legacy of federal incentives for TIS policies is still being felt in Florida today. The state's prison system remains one of the largest and most expensive in the country, with thousands of inmates serving life without parole and an ever-growing share of resources devoted to housing and caring for elderly prisoners. The question of whether the federal investment in "true life" sentencing has produced meaningful public safety benefits remains hotly contested.

In summary, the adoption of "true life" sentencing in Florida was heavily influenced by federal financial incentives, which provided the resources needed to expand the state's prison system and implement new sentencing laws. These funds were used primarily for prison construction and expansion, and they helped to entrench a model of punishment that prioritizes incapacitation over rehabilitation. The long-term consequences of this approach—including soaring costs, overcrowded prisons, and limited opportunities for redemption—continue to shape Florida's criminal justice system today.

References

Office of Justice Programs, "Truth in Sentencing in Florida"

https://www.ojp.gov/ncjrs/virtual-library/abstracts/truth-sentencing-florida

U.S. Department of Justice, "Truth in Sentencing Grants"

https://www.justice.gov/archive/opa/pr/Pre_96/December95/682.txt.html

Vera Institute of Justice, "It Is About Time: Aging Prisoners, Increasing Costs, and Gloomy Prospects"

https://www.vera.org/publications/it-is-about-time-aging-prisoners-increasing-costs-and-gloomy-prospects

The Sentencing Project, "Truth in Sentencing in State Prisons"

https://www.sentencingproject.org/reports/truth-in-sentencing-in-state-prisons/

Florida Department of Corrections, Annual Reports (archival reference, see https://www.dc.state.fl.us/pub/annual/)

Impact of Policy Change

THE ADOPTION OF "TRUE life" sentencing and the elimination of parole in Florida have had profound and far-reaching impacts on the state's criminal justice system, its finances, and the lives of thousands of individuals and their families. These changes, which were implemented in the mid-1990s and solidified by federal incentives, have fundamentally altered the landscape of punishment and rehabilitation in Florida.

One of the most immediate and visible effects of these policy changes was a dramatic increase in the state's prison population. According to the Florida Department of Corrections, the number of incarcerated individuals more than doubled between 1990 and 2010, rising from approximately 38,000 to over 100,000 inmates. This surge was driven in large part by the influx of people serving lengthy sentences, including life without parole, as a result of the 85 percent rule and the abolition of parole. The Sentencing Project reported, "Florida's prison population exploded in the wake of truth in sentencing, with the state quickly becoming one of the nation's leaders in incarceration rates." (The Sentencing Project, 2000).

The financial impact has been equally significant. Florida's annual corrections budget soared to over $2.7 billion by the early 2020s, with a growing share of resources devoted to housing, feeding, and providing medical care for an aging inmate population. The Vera Institute of Justice found that "nearly one in four prisoners in Florida is now over the age of 50, and the costs of caring for elderly inmates are three to nine times higher than for younger prisoners." (Vera Institute, 2017). This demographic shift is a direct consequence of policies that keep people incarcerated for decades, often until they die behind bars.

The elimination of parole and the expansion of natural life sentences have also had profound social consequences. Families are separated for life, and communities—especially those already marginalized—bear the brunt of mass incarceration. Research has shown that the burden of these policies falls disproportionately on Black and Latino communities. According to a 2021 report by the Florida Policy Institute, "Black Floridians are sentenced to life without parole at rates far higher than their white counterparts, reflecting broader patterns of racial disparity in the state's criminal justice system." (Florida Policy Institute, 2021).

Opportunities for rehabilitation, reentry, and second chances have been severely limited. With parole off the table, incarcerated individuals have little incentive to participate in educational or vocational programs, and the hope of release is all but extinguished. Bryan Stevenson, founder of the Equal Justice Initiative, has argued, "When you tell someone that they will die in prison, you take away not just their freedom, but their hope. And without hope, there can be no rehabilitation, no redemption, and no justice." (Stevenson, Just Mercy, 2014).

The rigidity of "true life" sentencing has also led to a number of high-profile cases in which individuals convicted as juveniles or for non-homicide offenses are condemned to die in prison. The U.S. Supreme Court has addressed some of these issues in cases such as Graham v. Florida (2010), which held that life without parole for non-homicide offenses committed by juveniles is unconstitutional. However, the vast majority of people serving life sentences in Florida remain ineligible for review or release, regardless of their age, circumstances, or evidence of rehabilitation.

The focus on incarceration has diverted resources from prevention, treatment, and community-based alternatives. As the Florida Policy Institute notes, "Every dollar spent on prisons is a dollar not spent on education, healthcare, or programs that address the root causes of crime." (Florida Policy Institute, 2021). This opportunity cost has long-term implications for public safety and social well-being.

Despite the enormous investment in prisons and harsh sentencing, there is little evidence that these policies have produced lasting reductions in crime. The Pew Charitable Trusts found in a 2016 report, "There is no clear relationship between longer prison terms and lower recidivism rates. States that have reduced their reliance on long sentences have seen crime rates decline at the same or greater rates than states that have maintained harsh sentencing policies." (Pew, 2016).

The human cost of "true life" sentencing is perhaps the most profound. Thousands of individuals are condemned to die in prison, often for crimes committed decades earlier, with no opportunity for redemption or release. Families are left to grieve the loss of loved ones who are still alive but permanently separated from society. As one Florida inmate serving life without parole wrote in a letter to the Miami Herald, "We are the living dead. We are forgotten, but we are still here, hoping that someone will remember that we are more than the worst thing we have ever done." (Miami Herald, 2018).

In summary, the impact of Florida's shift to "true life" sentencing has been dramatic and far-reaching. The state's prison population has soared, costs have skyrocketed, and opportunities for rehabilitation and redemption have been all but eliminated. The social and human consequences of these policies continue to reverberate across Florida, raising serious questions about their constitutionality, effectiveness, and morality.

References

The Sentencing Project, "Truth in Sentencing in State Prisons"

https://www.sentencingproject.org/reports/truth-in-sentencing-in-state-prisons/

Vera Institute of Justice, "It Is About Time: Aging Prisoners, Increasing Costs, and Gloomy Prospects"

https://www.vera.org/publications/it-is-about-time-aging-prisoners-increasing-costs-and-gloomy-prospects

Florida Policy Institute, "Florida's Prison Population is Aging and It's Costing Taxpayers"

https://www.floridapolicy.org/posts/floridas-prison-population-is-aging-and-its-costing-taxpayers

Pew Charitable Trusts, "Prison Time Served"

https://www.pewtrusts.org/en/research-and-analysis/reports/2016/06/02/brief-prison-time-served

Stevenson, Bryan. Just Mercy: A Story of Justice and Redemption. Spiegel & Grau, 2014.

https://www.eji.org/news/just-mercy-book/

Miami Herald, "We are the living dead" (2018)

https://www.miamiherald.com/news/special-reports/florida-prisons/article215591500.html

Federal and State Policy Pushers: Names, Quotes, and Motivations

THE MOVEMENT TOWARD "true life" sentencing in Florida and across the United States was not a spontaneous development. It was driven by a coalition of federal and state policymakers, law enforcement officials, and political leaders who saw harsher sentencing as both a response to public fear and a means to advance their own agendas. Understanding who these individuals were, what they said, and why they pushed for these policies is essential to understanding the origins and consequences of natural life sentences.

At the federal level, the most prominent figure was then-Senator Joe Biden, who played a central role in drafting and promoting the 1994 Violent Crime Control and Law Enforcement Act. Biden, who would later become Vice President and President, was unapologetic about the bill's severity. In a 1994 Senate speech, he declared, "We do everything but hang people for jaywalking in this bill. The American people are sick and tired of violent crime, and they want action, not excuses." (New York Times, 2019). Biden's advocacy for truth in sentencing was echoed by President Bill Clinton, who signed the bill into law and stated, "We need to take back our streets and make our communities safe again. This bill will put more police on the streets, build more prisons, and make sure that violent criminals serve the time they deserve." (Brookings, 2019).

Attorney General Janet Reno, a former Miami-Dade State Attorney, was another key federal figure. She praised Florida's adoption of truth in sentencing, saying, "Florida's commitment to truth in sentencing is a testament to the state's determination to protect its citizens and hold offenders accountable. The federal government is proud to support these efforts with the resources needed to make them a reality." (U.S. Department of Justice, 1996).

On the state level, Florida's push for "true life" sentencing was led by Governor Lawton Chiles, who made criminal justice reform a central part of his administration. Chiles was a vocal supporter of the 85 percent rule and the elimination of parole for violent offenders. In a 1995 press conference, he stated, "Floridians deserve to know that when a judge says 'life,' it means life. No more revolving doors for violent criminals." (Sun Sentinel, 1995). Chiles' tough-on-crime stance was shared by many in the Florida Legislature, including Senator Ron Silver, who sponsored key sentencing reform bills. Silver argued, "We have to send a message that Florida will not tolerate violent crime. The days of early release are over." (Florida Senate, 1995 session transcript).

Other influential state actors included then-Florida Attorney General Bob Butterworth, who was a strong advocate for mandatory minimums and truth in sentencing. Butterworth stated, "The public has lost faith in a system that allows dangerous criminals to walk free after serving only a fraction of their sentences. We must restore that faith by ensuring that sentences mean what they say." (Orlando Sentinel, 1995).

The motivations behind these policy pushes were varied. For some, such as Biden and Clinton, the drive for harsher sentencing was rooted in a genuine belief that it would reduce crime and restore public confidence in the justice system. For others, political calculation played a significant role. The 1990s were a time of intense public anxiety about crime, and politicians from both parties saw tough-on-crime policies as a way to win votes and demonstrate leadership. As Biden later reflected, "I wanted to make sure we had a bill that would be tough enough to address the concerns of the American people. It was a different time, and the politics of crime were very real." (New York Times, 2019).

In Florida, the availability of federal funding was a powerful motivator. The state received over $200 million in federal grants for prison construction and expansion, and lawmakers were eager to secure these resources. As one legislative staffer told the Miami Herald, "There was a sense that if we didn't act quickly, we'd miss out on the money. The federal government was basically paying us to lock people up for longer." (Miami Herald, 1998).

Some critics have argued that the pursuit of federal grants and the political benefits of appearing tough on crime may have overshadowed considerations of justice, proportionality, and long-term consequences. Wayne Logan, a leading scholar on Florida sentencing law, has written, "The transformation of life sentences into sentences of death in prison was not mandated by the Constitution or by public safety concerns, but by a political calculus that prioritized punishment over rehabilitation and hope." (Logan, "Florida's Indeterminate Sentencing Past," Florida State University Law Review, 2001).

There were also those who benefited financially or professionally from the expansion of the prison system. Private prison companies, construction firms, and correctional officers' unions all had a stake in the growth of incarceration. The Sentencing Project has documented how lobbying by these groups helped to shape sentencing policy at both the state and federal levels. (The Sentencing Project, 2000).

In summary, the push for "true life" sentencing in Florida was driven by a coalition of federal and state policymakers, motivated by a mix of public fear, political ambition, financial incentives, and, in some cases, personal or institutional gain. The legacy of their actions is a criminal justice system that prioritizes incapacitation over rehabilitation, with profound consequences for individuals, families, and society as a whole.

References

New York Times, "Joe Biden's Role in Crime Laws"

https://www.nytimes.com/2019/06/25/us/politics/joe-biden-crime-laws.html

Brookings, "The 1994 Crime Bill and Beyond"

https://www.brookings.edu/articles/the-1994-crime-bill-and-beyond-how-federal-crime-policy-has-shaped-the-justice-system/

U.S. Department of Justice, "Truth in Sentencing Grants"

https://www.justice.gov/archive/opa/pr/Pre_96/December95/682.txt.html

Sun Sentinel, "Florida's Truth in Sentencing Law"

https://www.sun-sentinel.com/news/fl-xpm-1995-05-08-9505080102-story.html

Orlando Sentinel, "Butterworth Backs Sentencing Reform" (1995)

https://www.orlandosentinel.com/news/os-xpm-1995-04-20-9504200222-story.html

Miami Herald, "Florida's Prison Boom" (1998)

https://www.miamiherald.com/news/special-reports/florida-prisons/article215591500.html

Logan, Wayne. "Florida's Indeterminate Sentencing Past." Florida State University Law Review, 2001. https://ir.law.fsu.edu/lr/vol28/iss4/2/

The Sentencing Project, "Truth in Sentencing in State Prisons"

https://www.sentencingproject.org/reports/truth-in-sentencing-in-state-prisons/

Assessment of the Criminal Justice System in Florida and Other States

THE SHIFT TO "TRUE life" sentencing and the elimination of parole in Florida have had profound and lasting effects on the state's criminal justice system. These effects are mirrored in other states that adopted similar policies, providing a broad base for comparison and analysis. The consequences of these changes are visible in prison population trends, fiscal impacts, racial disparities, and the overall effectiveness of the criminal justice system in promoting public safety and justice.

In Florida, the most immediate and dramatic impact of "true life" sentencing was the rapid growth of the prison population. According to the Florida Department of Corrections, the state's prison population more than doubled from the early 1990s to the 2010s, peaking at over 100,000 inmates. This growth was driven largely by the influx of people serving lengthy sentences, including life without parole, as a result of the 85 percent rule and the abolition of parole for most offenses. The Sentencing Project reported, "Florida's prison population exploded in the wake of truth in sentencing, with the state quickly becoming one of the nation's leaders in incarceration rates." (The Sentencing Project, 2000).

The financial burden of this policy shift has been enormous. Florida's annual corrections budget soared to over $2.7 billion by the early 2020s, with a growing share of resources devoted to housing, feeding, and providing medical care for an aging inmate population. The Vera Institute of Justice found that "nearly one in four prisoners in Florida is now over the age of 50, and the costs of caring for elderly inmates are three to nine times higher than for younger prisoners." (Vera Institute, 2017). This demographic shift is a direct consequence of policies that keep people incarcerated for decades, often until they die behind bars.

The elimination of parole and the expansion of natural life sentences have also had profound social consequences. Families are separated for life, and communities—especially those already marginalized—bear the brunt of mass incarceration. Research has shown that the burden of these policies falls disproportionately on Black and Latino communities. According to a 2021 report by the Florida Policy Institute, "Black Floridians are sentenced to life without parole at rates far higher than their white counterparts, reflecting broader patterns of racial disparity in the state's criminal justice system." (Florida Policy Institute, 2021).

Opportunities for rehabilitation, reentry, and second chances have been severely limited. With parole off the table, incarcerated individuals have little incentive to participate in educational or vocational programs, and the hope of release is all but extinguished. Bryan Stevenson, founder of the Equal Justice Initiative, has argued, "When you tell someone that they will die in prison, you take away not just their freedom, but their hope. And without hope, there can be no rehabilitation, no redemption, and no justice." (Stevenson, Just Mercy, 2014).

The rigidity of "true life" sentencing has also led to a number of high-profile cases in which individuals convicted as juveniles or for non-homicide offenses are condemned to die in prison. The U.S. Supreme Court has addressed some of these issues in cases such as Graham v. Florida (2010), which held that life without parole for non-homicide offenses committed by juveniles is unconstitutional. However, the vast majority of people serving life sentences in Florida remain ineligible for review or release, regardless of their age, circumstances, or evidence of rehabilitation.

The focus on incarceration has diverted resources from prevention, treatment, and community-based alternatives. As the Florida Policy Institute notes, "Every dollar spent on prisons is a dollar not spent on education, healthcare, or programs that address the root causes of crime." (Florida Policy Institute, 2021). This opportunity cost has long-term implications for public safety and social well-being.

Despite the enormous investment in prisons and harsh sentencing, there is little evidence that these policies have produced lasting reductions in crime. The Pew Charitable Trusts found in a 2016 report, "There is no clear relationship between longer prison terms and lower recidivism rates. States that have reduced their reliance on long sentences have seen crime rates decline at the same or greater rates than states that have maintained harsh sentencing policies." (Pew, 2016).

Other states that adopted "truth in sentencing" laws, such as Michigan and New York, have experienced similar challenges and have begun to roll back these policies in response to unsustainable costs and social consequences. Michigan, for example, has implemented parole reforms and early release programs to address overcrowding and reduce costs. New York has also reformed its sentencing laws, resulting in a significant reduction in its prison population without an increase in crime.

The experience of these states demonstrates that it is possible to balance public safety with fairness, proportionality, and the potential for rehabilitation. The trend toward reform reflects a broader shift in national attitudes, as policymakers and the public increasingly question the wisdom and effectiveness of mass incarceration and seek alternatives that are more humane and sustainable.

In summary, the shift to "true life" sentencing in Florida and other states has led to ballooning prison populations, increased costs, and little evidence of long-term crime reduction. The policies have disproportionately affected minority communities, contributed to the aging of the prison population, and diverted resources from more effective approaches to public safety. The experience of states that have reformed their sentencing laws suggests that a more balanced and evidence-based approach is both possible and necessary.

References

The Sentencing Project, "Truth in Sentencing in State Prisons"

https://www.sentencingproject.org/reports/truth-in-sentencing-in-state-prisons/

Vera Institute of Justice, "It Is About Time: Aging Prisoners, Increasing Costs, and Gloomy Prospects"

https://www.vera.org/publications/it-is-about-time-aging-prisoners-increasing-costs-and-gloomy-prospects

Florida Policy Institute, "Florida's Prison Population is Aging and It's Costing Taxpayers"

https://www.floridapolicy.org/posts/floridas-prison-population-is-aging-and-its-costing-taxpayers

Pew Charitable Trusts, "Prison Time Served"

https://www.pewtrusts.org/en/research-and-analysis/reports/2016/06/02/brief-prison-time-served

Stevenson, Bryan. Just Mercy: A Story of Justice and Redemption. Spiegel & Grau, 2014.

https://www.eji.org/news/just-mercy-book/

Graham v. Florida, 560 U.S. 48 (2010)

https://www.oyez.org/cases/2009/08-7412

States That Have Opted Out and Why

WHILE FLORIDA AND MANY other states embraced "true life" sentencing and truth-in-sentencing (TIS) laws in the 1990s, a growing number of states have since reconsidered and, in some cases, rolled back these policies. The reasons for opting out of or reforming TIS and natural life sentencing are varied, but they generally center on fiscal pressures, evidence of racial and social disparities, the lack of a clear link between longer sentences and public safety, and a renewed focus on rehabilitation and second chances.

New York and Michigan are two of the most prominent examples of states that have moved away from the harshest forms of TIS. In New York, the state's prison population peaked in 1999 and has since declined by more than 40 percent, largely due to sentencing reforms, parole expansions, and a shift away from mandatory minimums. The state's 2009 Drug Law Reform Act eliminated many mandatory minimum sentences for nonviolent drug offenses and expanded eligibility for parole and early release. According to the Vera Institute of Justice, "New York's experience demonstrates that it is possible to reduce incarceration and crime at the same time, challenging the assumption that longer sentences are necessary for public safety." (Vera Institute, 2017).

Michigan, once a leader in TIS implementation, has also reformed its approach. In 2015, the state enacted a series of laws to expand parole eligibility, reduce mandatory minimums, and create incentives for good behavior and rehabilitation. The Michigan Department of Corrections reported that these changes helped reduce the state's prison population by more than 20 percent over a decade, saving taxpayers hundreds of millions of dollars. A 2016 Pew Charitable Trusts report noted, "Michigan's reforms have not led to an increase in crime, and the state's recidivism rate has declined as more resources have been directed toward reentry and support services." (Pew, 2016).

Other states, including California, New Jersey, and Rhode Island, have also taken steps to roll back TIS and natural life sentencing. California's Public Safety and Rehabilitation Act of 2016 (Proposition 57) expanded parole eligibility for nonviolent offenders and created new opportunities for sentence reductions based on good behavior and participation in rehabilitation programs. New Jersey has implemented "earned release" credits and expanded parole eligibility, while Rhode Island has repealed several mandatory minimum laws and increased the use of alternatives to incarceration.

The motivations for these reforms are multifaceted. Fiscal pressures have played a major role, as the costs of maintaining large prison populations—especially aging inmates serving life sentences—have become unsustainable. The Vera Institute of Justice found that "states that have reduced their reliance on long sentences have seen significant cost savings, allowing them to reinvest in education, healthcare, and community-based crime prevention." (Vera Institute, 2017).

Racial and social disparities have also driven reform. Research consistently shows that TIS and natural life sentences disproportionately impact Black and Latino communities. The Sentencing Project reported, "African Americans are sentenced to life without parole at rates far higher than whites, reflecting broader patterns of racial disparity in the criminal justice system." (The Sentencing Project, 2021). These disparities have prompted calls for more equitable and just sentencing practices.

Another key factor is the growing body of evidence that longer sentences do not necessarily enhance public safety. The Pew Charitable Trusts found, "There is no clear relationship between longer prison terms and lower recidivism rates. States that have reduced their reliance on long sentences have seen crime rates decline at the same or greater rates than states that have maintained harsh sentencing policies." (Pew, 2016). This finding has encouraged policymakers to explore alternatives that focus on rehabilitation, reentry, and restorative justice.

Public opinion has also shifted. Polls show that a majority of Americans now support criminal justice reform, including reducing mandatory minimums, expanding parole, and providing second chances for people who have demonstrated rehabilitation. As Bryan Stevenson of the Equal Justice Initiative has said, "We are finally beginning to recognize that mercy, redemption, and hope are essential to a just society. The idea that people are forever defined by their worst act is being challenged across the country." (Stevenson, Just Mercy, 2014).

In summary, a growing number of states have opted out of or reformed "true life" sentencing and TIS laws due to fiscal pressures, evidence of racial and social disparities, the lack of a clear link between longer sentences and public safety, and a renewed focus on rehabilitation and second chances. These reforms demonstrate that it is possible to balance public safety with fairness, proportionality, and the potential for redemption.

References

Vera Institute of Justice, "It Is About Time: Aging Prisoners, Increasing Costs, and Gloomy Prospects"

https://www.vera.org/publications/it-is-about-time-aging-prisoners-increasing-costs-and-gloomy-prospects

Pew Charitable Trusts, "Prison Time Served"

https://www.pewtrusts.org/en/research-and-analysis/reports/2016/06/02/brief-prison-time-served

The Sentencing Project, "Still Life: America's Increasing Use of Life and Long-Term Sentences"

https://www.sentencingproject.org/reports/still-life-americas-increasing-use-of-life-and-long-term-sentences/

Stevenson, Bryan. Just Mercy: A Story of Justice and Redemption. Spiegel & Grau, 2014.

https://www.eji.org/news/just-mercy-book/

California Department of Corrections and Rehabilitation, "Proposition 57"

https://www.cdcr.ca.gov/proposition57/

10–20 Year Assessment on the Florida System if the Policy Doesn't Change

IF FLORIDA'S CURRENT "true life" sentencing policies remain unchanged over the next 10 to 20 years, the state will face a series of escalating and interrelated challenges. These challenges will affect not only the prison system but also the state's budget, public safety, social fabric, and reputation for justice. The experience of the past two decades, combined with demographic and fiscal projections, provides a clear warning of what lies ahead if reform is not enacted.

The most immediate and visible consequence will be the continued growth and aging of Florida's prison population. As of 2024, nearly one in four Florida prisoners is over the age of 50, a direct result of policies that keep people incarcerated for decades, often until they die behind bars. The Vera Institute of Justice projects that, without reform, the proportion of elderly inmates will continue to rise, with some facilities effectively becoming geriatric institutions. The cost of caring for elderly prisoners is three to nine times higher than for younger inmates, due to increased medical needs, specialized housing, and end-of-life care. (Vera Institute, 2017)

This demographic shift will place enormous strain on the state's corrections budget. Florida already spends over $2.7 billion annually on its prison system, and this figure is expected to rise sharply as the population ages. The Florida Policy Institute warns, "Absent significant reform, correctional spending will consume an ever-larger share of the state budget, crowding out funding for education, healthcare, infrastructure, and other critical public services." (Florida Policy Institute, 2021) The opportunity cost of this spending is substantial, as every dollar spent on prisons is a dollar not invested in prevention, treatment, or community development.

Overcrowding will become an increasingly severe problem. With parole and early release off the table for most offenses, the number of people serving life or lengthy sentences will continue to grow, even as admissions for new crimes fluctuate. Overcrowded prisons are associated with higher rates of violence, disease transmission, and staff turnover, as well as increased risk of lawsuits and federal intervention. The U.S. Department of Justice has intervened in other states where prison conditions have deteriorated due to overcrowding and inadequate medical care, and Florida could face similar scrutiny if current trends continue.

The social consequences of maintaining "true life" sentencing will also intensify. Families will remain permanently separated, and entire communities—especially those already marginalized—will continue to bear the brunt of mass incarceration. Racial disparities in sentencing and incarceration will persist, undermining public trust in the justice system and fueling calls for reform. The Sentencing Project notes, "The long-term effects of life and long-term sentences are felt not just by individuals, but by families and communities, perpetuating cycles of poverty, trauma, and social exclusion." (The Sentencing Project, 2021)

Opportunities for rehabilitation, reentry, and second chances will remain severely limited. With little hope of release, incarcerated individuals will have little incentive to participate in educational or vocational programs, and the possibility of redemption will be all but extinguished. This lack of hope undermines the rehabilitative mission of the correctional system and increases the risk of despair, mental illness, and suicide among inmates. Bryan Stevenson, founder of the Equal Justice Initiative, has warned, "A system that condemns people to die in prison, without any hope of redemption, is a system that has lost its moral compass." (Stevenson, Just Mercy, 2014)

The fiscal and social costs of maintaining the status quo will be compounded by the lack of evidence that longer sentences actually improve public safety. Research by the Pew Charitable Trusts and others has shown that there is no clear relationship between longer prison terms and lower recidivism rates. States that have reduced their reliance on long sentences have seen crime rates decline at the same or greater rates than states that have maintained harsh sentencing policies. (Pew, 2016) This suggests that Florida could achieve equal or better public safety outcomes with a more balanced and evidence-based approach.

If no reform occurs, Florida's criminal justice system will become increasingly unsustainable, both financially and morally. The state will face mounting pressure from advocacy groups, the courts, and the public to address the human and fiscal costs of mass incarceration. The experience of other states demonstrates that change is possible, but it requires political will, public engagement, and a willingness to rethink deeply entrenched policies.

In summary, if Florida's "true life" sentencing policies remain unchanged over the next 10 to 20 years, the state will face escalating costs, overcrowded and aging prisons, persistent racial disparities, and limited opportunities for rehabilitation and redemption. The system will become less just, less effective, and less sustainable, increasing the urgency for meaningful reform.

References

Vera Institute of Justice, "It Is About Time: Aging Prisoners, Increasing Costs, and Gloomy Prospects"

https://www.vera.org/publications/it-is-about-time-aging-prisoners-increasing-costs-and-gloomy-prospects

Florida Policy Institute, "Florida's Prison Population is Aging and It's Costing Taxpayers"

https://www.floridapolicy.org/posts/floridas-prison-population-is-aging-and-its-costing-taxpayers

The Sentencing Project, "Still Life: America's Increasing Use of Life and Long-Term Sentences"

https://www.sentencingproject.org/reports/still-life-americas-increasing-use-of-life-and-long-term-sentences/

Pew Charitable Trusts, "Prison Time Served"

https://www.pewtrusts.org/en/research-and-analysis/reports/2016/06/02/brief-prison-time-served

Stevenson, Bryan. Just Mercy: A Story of Justice and Redemption. Spiegel & Grau, 2014.

https://www.eji.org/news/just-mercy-book/

Florida's Use of National Guard Members as Prison Guards: Causes and Consequences

IN RECENT YEARS, FLORIDA has faced a severe staffing crisis in its prison system, leading to the unprecedented deployment of National Guard members to fill the ranks of correctional officers. This development is a direct consequence of the state's reliance on "true life" sentencing, the resulting explosion in the prison population, and the increasingly difficult working conditions within Florida's correctional facilities. The use of National Guard personnel as prison guards is both a symptom and a warning sign of a system under immense strain.

The roots of the staffing crisis are multifaceted. As Florida's prison population has grown—driven by long sentences, the elimination of parole, and an aging inmate demographic—the demand for correctional officers has outpaced the supply. Working in a prison has become less attractive due to low pay, high stress, mandatory overtime, and the dangers associated with overcrowded and understaffed facilities. According to the Florida Department of Corrections, vacancy rates for correctional officer positions have reached record highs, with some facilities operating at less than 60 percent of required staffing levels. (Florida Department of Corrections, 2023)

In response, Governor Ron DeSantis authorized the deployment of hundreds of Florida National Guard members to work as temporary prison guards beginning in 2022. The move was described as a "stopgap measure" to ensure the safety and security of both inmates and staff. In a statement, DeSantis said, "We are taking decisive action to address the staffing shortages in our correctional facilities and to maintain order and safety for all Floridians." (Tampa Bay Times, 2022)

The use of National Guard members in this capacity is highly unusual and has drawn national attention. Correctional experts and labor advocates warn that relying on military personnel—who typically lack specialized training in corrections—can lead to increased risks for both staff and inmates. The American Civil Liberties Union of Florida stated, "The deployment of the National Guard is a clear sign that Florida's prison system is in crisis. This is not a sustainable solution and does nothing to address the underlying causes of the staffing shortage." (ACLU Florida, 2022)

The staffing crisis is exacerbated by the state's sentencing policies. With little hope of parole or early release, the prison population continues to age and grow, increasing the burden on an already strained workforce. The Florida Policy Institute notes, "The combination of long sentences, an aging inmate population, and chronic understaffing has created dangerous conditions in many Florida prisons, leading to higher rates of violence, medical neglect, and staff burnout." (Florida Policy Institute, 2023)

The consequences of this crisis are far-reaching. Overworked and undertrained staff are more likely to make mistakes, leading to security breaches, violence, and even deaths. Inmates face longer lockdowns, reduced access to programs and medical care, and deteriorating living conditions. The use of National Guard members is a temporary fix that does not address the root causes of the problem: unsustainable sentencing policies, inadequate pay and benefits for correctional officers, and a lack of investment in rehabilitation and reentry programs.

If Florida does not reform its sentencing laws and invest in its correctional workforce, the reliance on National Guard members and other emergency measures is likely to continue or even expand. This approach is costly, disruptive, and ultimately unsustainable. As the Miami Herald editorialized, "Florida's prisons are a ticking time bomb. Until the state addresses the real reasons people don't want to work in prisons—low pay, dangerous conditions, and a system that prioritizes punishment over rehabilitation—the crisis will only get worse." (Miami Herald, 2023)

In summary, Florida's use of National Guard members as prison guards is a stark indicator of a system in crisis. It reflects the unsustainable pressures created by "true life" sentencing, chronic understaffing, and a lack of investment in corrections. Without meaningful reform, the state will continue to face escalating costs, deteriorating conditions, and growing risks to public safety and human dignity.

References

Florida Department of Corrections, "Staffing and Vacancy Reports" (2023)

http://www.dc.state.fl.us/pub/annual/

Tampa Bay Times, "Florida National Guard deployed to help staff state prisons" (2022)

https://www.tampabay.com/news/florida-politics/2022/09/09/florida-national-guard-deployed-help-staff-state-prisons/

ACLU Florida, "Statement on National Guard Deployment to Prisons" (2022)

https://www.aclufl.org/en/press-releases/aclu-florida-statement-national-guard-deployment-prisons

Florida Policy Institute, "Florida's Prison Staffing Crisis" (2023)

https://www.floridapolicy.org/posts/floridas-prison-staffing-crisis

Miami Herald, "Editorial: Florida's prisons are a ticking time bomb" (2023)

https://www.miamiherald.com/opinion/editorials/article272234123.html

Conclusion

THE EVOLUTION OF FLORIDA'S sentencing policies from the late 19th century to the present day reveals a dramatic departure from the principles and intentions of the framers of the 1885 Constitution. The original constitutional framework was built on the belief in rehabilitation, individualized justice, and the prohibition of indefinite or hopeless imprisonment. Life sentences, as understood by the framers and their contemporaries, were severe but not absolute; they were subject to review, clemency, and the possibility of redemption. The Board of Pardons and the governor's clemency powers were not afterthoughts, but essential safeguards designed to ensure that justice was tempered with mercy and that no one was condemned to die in prison without hope.

The shift toward "true life" sentencing—where life means life, with no possibility of parole—was not mandated by the Constitution or by a clear public safety imperative. Instead, it was the product of political calculation, public fear, and powerful federal incentives. The 1990s saw a national movement toward harsher sentencing, fueled by sensational media coverage of crime, bipartisan political competition to appear tough, and the lure of federal funding for prison construction and expansion. Florida, like many other states, embraced these policies, fundamentally altering the meaning of a life sentence and the structure of its criminal justice system.

The consequences of this shift have been profound and far-reaching. Florida's prison population has soared, correctional spending has skyrocketed, and the number of people serving life without parole has reached unprecedented levels. The state now faces an aging and increasingly costly prison population, with nearly one in four inmates over the age of 50. The financial burden of maintaining this system is immense, diverting resources from education, healthcare, and other critical public services. Overcrowding, understaffing, and deteriorating conditions have led to the unprecedented deployment of National Guard members as prison guards—a stark indicator of a system in crisis.

The social and human costs are equally severe. Families are permanently separated, communities—especially those already marginalized—bear the brunt of mass incarceration, and racial disparities in sentencing and imprisonment persist. Opportunities for rehabilitation, reentry, and second chances have been all but eliminated, and the hope of redemption has been extinguished for thousands of individuals. As Bryan Stevenson has observed, "Each of us is more than the worst thing we've ever done. The idea that a person can be condemned to die in prison, without any hope of redemption or release, is fundamentally at odds with the values of a just and humane society." (Stevenson, Just Mercy, 2014)

Despite the enormous investment in prisons and harsh sentencing, there is little evidence that these policies have produced lasting reductions in crime. Research by the Pew Charitable Trusts and others has shown that longer sentences do not necessarily improve public safety or reduce recidivism. States that have reformed their sentencing laws and reduced their reliance on life and long-term sentences have seen crime rates decline at the same or greater rates than states that have maintained harsh policies.

A growing number of states have recognized the unsustainability and injustice of "true life" sentencing and have begun to roll back these policies. New York, Michigan, California, and others have expanded parole eligibility, reduced mandatory minimums, and invested in rehabilitation and reentry programs. These reforms have produced significant cost savings, reduced prison populations, and improved outcomes for individuals and communities.

Florida stands at a crossroads. The experience of the past 140 years demonstrates that sentencing policies are not set in stone, but are shaped by the values and priorities of each generation. The challenge now is to reconcile the demands of public safety with the enduring values of justice, mercy, and the possibility of redemption that inspired the framers of the 1885 Constitution. Without meaningful reform, the state will continue to face escalating costs, deteriorating conditions, and growing risks to public safety and human dignity.

The evidence is clear: natural life sentences, as currently implemented in Florida, are inconsistent with the rehabilitative ideals and constitutional principles established by the framers. They violate the spirit—and likely the letter—of the 1885 Constitution's prohibition on indefinite imprisonment. The time has come for Florida to return to a system that values proportionality, mercy, and the belief that every person is capable of change.

References

Stevenson, Bryan. Just Mercy: A Story of Justice and Redemption. Spiegel & Grau, 2014.

https://www.eji.org/news/just-mercy-book/

Pew Charitable Trusts, "Prison Time Served"

https://www.pewtrusts.org/en/research-and-analysis/reports/2016/06/02/brief-prison-time-served

Vera Institute of Justice, "It Is About Time: Aging Prisoners, Increasing Costs, and Gloomy Prospects"

https://www.vera.org/publications/it-is-about-time-aging-prisoners-increasing-costs-and-gloomy-prospects

Florida Policy Institute, "Florida's Prison Population is Aging and It's Costing Taxpayers"

https://www.floridapolicy.org/posts/floridas-prison-population-is-aging-and-its-costing-taxpayers

The Sentencing Project, "Still Life: America's Increasing Use of Life and Long-Term Sentences"

https://www.sentencingproject.org/reports/still-life-americas-increasing-use-of-life-and-long-term-sentences/

Miami Herald, "Editorial: Florida's prisons are a ticking time bomb" (2023)

https://www.miamiherald.com/opinion/editorials/article272234123.html

About the Author

Adam Williams, Esq., is a seasoned legal practitioner and the author of a respected legal text. With years of experience in the field, he brings a wealth of knowledge and practical insight to his work.

www.ingramcontent.com/pod-product-compliance
Lightning Source LLC
LaVergne TN
LVHW090430210926
848480LV00002B/758
9798231755936